MW01122876

vol. 3

by
Marie-France Marcie
Music by Sara Jordan

Produced and Published by
Sara Jordan Publishing
a division of ℗©2006 Jordan Music Productions Inc.
(SOCAN)

ISBN 1-55386-045-4

Acknowledgments

Lyricist - Marie-France Marcie
Editor - Véronique Ponce
Composer and Producer - Sara Jordan
Music Co-producer, Arranger, Engineer - Mark Shannon
Male Singer - Peter LeBuis
Female Singer - Julie Crochetière
Illustrations - Jessica Jordan-Brough
Cover Design and Layout - Campbell Creative Services

Digitally Recorded and Mixed by Mark Shannon,
The TreeFort, Toronto, Ontario.

For further information contact:

Jordan Music Productions Inc.
M.P.O. Box 490
Niagara Falls, NY
U.S.A. 14302-0490

Jordan Music Productions Inc.
Station M, Box 160
Toronto, Ontario
Canada, M6S 4T3

Internet: http://www.sara-jordan.com
e-mail: sjordan@sara-jordan.com
Telephone: (800) 567-7733

To the children of the world who want to learn!

Aux enfants du monde entier qui veulent apprendre!

Recommended Companion

We suggest purchasing our campanion resource book, *Bilingual Kids English-French, vol. 3*, which has lessons, activities and reproducible exercises reinforcing the material taught in these songs.

For more information please visit www.SongsThatTeach.com

or call us toll free
1-800-567-7733

The translation of these bilingual songs is close in most cases, however, in some verses similar words and arrangement of the words were used to obtain better musical results.

We acknowledge the financial support of the Government of Canada through the Book Publishing Industry Development Program (BPIDP) for our publishing activities.

Contents / *Table des matières*

Hints for Teachers and Parents

Bilingual Songs: English-French, vol. 3 has been developed for use by second language learners as well as instructors, parents and teachers.

These songs, featuring curriculum based content, offer an attractive and easy-to-use format that facilitates learning in French and English.

Complying with the five major principles of the Standards of Foreign Language Learning: *Communication, Culture, Connections, Comparisons,* and *Communities,* these bilingual songs integrate skill development through exciting rhythms and melodies that also provide a real-world context for cultural understanding.

Students will improve literacy, vocabulary, reading, and comprehension skills through the use of this book of lyrics, rules and examples. This program works well for learners with diverse learning styles, backgrounds, and disciplines. The lessons can be carried into many areas of study, and more importantly, go beyond the classroom and become part of students' lives at home and in the community.

Enjoy it! *Amusez-vous!*

This learning kit has three components: an audio CD, a 48 page lyrics book and an optional 64 page resource book. They can be used separately, however, if used in tandem, better results will be obtained.

All of the songs in this volume can be used to teach either French or English. Song 12 concentrates on the different rules for capitalization in each language. The bonus instrumental tracks, which are included on the CD, further boost language fluency as students use the lyrics book to perform "karaoke" style.

A few ways to use this resource:

This resource works well as both a remedial tutorial and as an enriching curriculum supplement:

In the classroom:

- ☑ Have beginning students listen while using the lyrics book. Later have them sing along.

- ☑ Encourage confident students to perform karaoke style with the music accompaniment tracks.

- ☑ Advanced students may use the music tracks to create and perform original lyrics (boosting their writing skills).

- ☑ Employ the "cloze" method of learning by "whiting out" some of the words (using a photocopied sheet of lyrics) and have students fill in the words while listening.

At home or in the car:

- ☑ Whether you listen on the family stereo, through a stereo headset, or in the car, *Bilingual Songs: English-French, vol. 3* can be great fun and entertainment for the entire family.

Introduction
L'introduction

chorus/*refrain 2x* :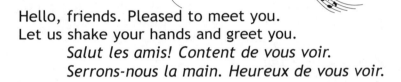

Hello, friends. Pleased to meet you.
Let us shake your hands and greet you.
> *Salut les amis! Content de vous voir.*
> *Serrons-nous la main. Heureux de vous voir.*

We'll have fun
as we sing along
to Volume 3
of 'Bilingual Songs'.

On va s'amuser
en chantant
Volume 3
de «Bilingual Songs».

These songs teach
so many things;
but to learn them,
we must sing.

On apprend tout
avec ces chansons
et pour tout savoir
nous chantons.

chorus/*refrain 2x* :

Nº 2

Pleased to Meet You!
Content de vous voir!

I am Mr. Lebois.
I am Miss Shelton.
I am Mrs. Lacroix.
Pleased to meet you! *Content de vous voir!*

Bonjour, M. Lebois.
Bonjour, Mlle Shelton.
Bonjour, Mme Lacroix.
Pleased to meet you! *Content de vous voir!*

Je m'appelle Dr. Martin.
Je m'appelle Mlle Dupont.
Je m'appelle Mme Marcie.
Pleased to meet you! *Content de vous voir!*

Hello, Dr. Martin.
Hello, Miss Dupont.
Hello, Mrs. Marcie.
Pleased to meet you! *Content de vous voir!*

Thank you for this song.
Sorry we must move along.
You are very welcome.
Pleased to meet you! *Content de vous voir!*

Merci pour cette chanson.
Mais avancer nous devons.
Bienvenue, de rien.
Pleased to meet you! *Content de vous voir!*

Good-bye, Mr. Lebois.
Good-bye, Miss Shelton.
Good-bye, Mrs. Lacroix.
Pleased to meet you! *Content de vous voir!*

Au revoir, Dr. Martin
Au revoir, Mlle Dupont.
Au revoir, Mme Marcie.
Pleased to meet you! *Content de vous voir!*

Remember the Gender
Attention au genre

chorus/*refrain* :

"Remember the gender
when you're speaking French.
In French we say 'le' or 'la'
In English only 'the'."

> «*N'oubliez pas le genre*
> *en parlant français.*
> *En français on dit ‹le› ou ‹la›*
> *en anglais seulement ‹the›.*»

My teacher said, "This morning we have
lots of work to do.
We need a list of inventory
when the day is through.

So look around and memorize
everything you see.
Write it down. Make a list.
Then give it to me."

chorus/refrain...

Ma professeure dit, «Ce matin
nous avons beaucoup à faire.
Nous avons besoin d'une liste
pour notre inventaire.

Regardez partout. Retenez
tout ce que vous voyez.
Écrivez. Faites une liste
et à moi vous la donnez.»

chorus/refrain...

the calendar	le calendrier
the dictionary	le dictionnaire
the pen	le stylo
the notebook	le cahier
the book	le livre
the backpack	le sac à dos
Sing with me.	Chantez!
One, two, three.	

chorus/*refrain*...

the chair	*la chaise*
the bin	*la poubelle*
the table	*la table*
the chalk	*la craie*
the window	*la fenêtre*
the ruler	*la règle*
Chantez avec moi!	Sing!
Un, deux, trois.	

chorus/*refrain*...

Articles
Les articles

chorus/*refrain 2x :*

Le, la, ou les?
Choosing one can be tough.
Un, une, ou des?
Choosing can be rough.

> *Le, la, ou les?*
> *C'est dificile de choisir.*
> *Un, une, ou des?*
> *C'est risqué de choisir.*

Definite articles
show
if a noun is specific
or it's known.

> *L'article défini*
> *indique*
> *si un nom est connu*
> *ou spécifique.*

Indefinite articles
show
if a noun is general
or unknown.

L'article indéfini
indique
si un nom est inconnu
ou non spécifique.

chorus/*refrain*...

Here are some examples!
Voici quelques exemples!

Lucie wants <u>a</u> teddy bear.
She wants <u>the</u> big teddy bear.
Rose wants <u>a</u> doll.
She wants <u>the</u> princess doll.

Lucie veut <u>un</u> ours en peluche.
Elle veut <u>le</u> gros ours en peluche.
Rose veut <u>une</u> poupée.
Elle veut <u>la</u> belle poupée.

Jacques wants <u>some</u> marbles.
He wants <u>the</u> white marbles.
Guy wants <u>some</u> balloons.
He wants <u>the</u> red balloons.

Jacques veut <u>des</u> billes.
Il veut <u>les</u> billes blanches.
Guy veut <u>des</u> ballons.
Il veut <u>les</u> ballons rouges.

chorus/*refrain 2x* :

 Bilingual Songs - ENGLISH-FRENCH vol. 3   © 2006 Sara Jordan Publishing

Nº 5

Plurals in the Circus
Le pluriel, quel cirque

chorus/*refrain* :

Changing singular to plural
    Changer du singulier au pluriel
is sometimes tricky I confess.
    est dificile je le confesse.
In English there are several endings:
    En anglais voici les terminaisons :
    's', 'es', or, 'ies'
    «*s*», «*es*», *ou* «*ies*».

Changing singular to plural
    Changer du singulier au pluriel
is sometimes tricky I confess.
    est dificile je le confesse.
French endings differ slightly:
    En français voici les terminaisons :
We use either 'x' or 's'.
    On utilise soit «*x*» *ou* «*s*».

Welcome to the circus where
magicians do their tricks
and where one thing becomes many
with the waving of a stick.

*Bienvenue au cirque où
les magiciens font leurs tours,
où une chose se multiplie
d'un coup de baguette magique.*

A bunny becomes bunnies,
a monkey becomes monkeys,
a lion becomes lions,
and a lynx becomes lynxes.

*Un lapin devient des lapins,
un babouin devient des babouins,
un lionceau devient des lionceaux,
et un lynx devient des lynx.*

chorus/*refrain*...

The endings that we choose
depend on the nouns we use.
    *Les terminaisons utilisées
    dépendent des noms employés.*

Some rules / *Quelques règles*

Le pluriel des noms en anglais :

Pour former le pluriel on ajoute en général un «s» :
lion = lions

Si le nom se termine par -o, -s, -ss, -x, -sh, -ch on ajoute «es» :
lynx = lynxes

Si le nom finit par une consonne et un «y», changez le «y» en «i» et ajoutez «es» :
bunny = bunnies

Plural of French nouns:

If the noun ends in a vowel add 's':
le magicien = les magiciens

If the noun ends with 's', 'z' or 'x' there is no change:
le lynx = les lynx

If the noun ends in 'eau' add 'x':
le lionceau = les lionceaux

N° 6

Dates
La date

chorus:

In English we use ordinal numbers
when we say the date.
For example: April 1st
and July 8th.

In French we use cardinal numbers
except for the first of the month.
For example: *le 1er avril*
and *le 8 juillet*.

My birthday is on May 1st.
Mon anniversaire est le 1er mai.
Paul's birthday is on April 2nd.
L'anniversaire de Paul est le 2 avril.

Luc's birthday is on June 3rd.
L'anniversaire de Luc est le 3 juin.
Marie's birthday is on July 4th.
L'anniversaire de Marie est le 4 juillet.

refrain :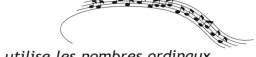

On utilise les nombres ordinaux
pour dire la date en anglais.
Par exemple : April 1st
et July 8th.

En français on utilise les nombres cardinaux
sauf pour le premier jour du mois.
Par exemple : le 1er avril
et le 8 juillet.

'in' and 'on'
Prepositions are tricky.
My birthday is 'in' May.
It's 'on' May 6th.

«In» et «on»
en anglais sont compliqués.
Mon anniversaire est «in» May.
C'est «on» May 6th.

«En» and *«le»*
In French these are tricky.
My birthday is *«en» avril.*
C'est «le» 6 avril.

«En» et «le»
en français sont difficiles.
Mon anniversaire est «en avril».
C'est le 6 avril.

chorus / refrain :

In English we use ordinal numbers
when we say the date.
For example: 'April 1st'
and 'July 8th'.

In French we use cardinal numbers
except for the first of the month.
For example: *«le 1er avril»*
and *«le 8 juillet»*.

On utilise les nombres ordinaux
pour dire la date en anglais.
Par exemple : «April 1st»
et «July 8th».

En français on utilise les nombres cardinaux
sauf pour le premier jour du mois.
Par exemple : «le 1er avril»
et «le 8 juillet».

Some rules / *Quelques règles*

Cardinal and Ordinal Numbers / *Les nombres ordinaux et cardinaux*

un	premier	1	one	first
deux	deuxième	2	two	second
trois	troisième	3	three	third
quatre	quatrième	4	four	fourth
cinq	cinqième	5	five	fifth
six	sixième	6	six	sixth
sept	septième	7	seven	seventh
huit	huitième	8	eight	eighth
neuf	neuvième	9	nine	ninth
dix	dixième	10	ten	tenth

NOTE: For more information and exercises please consult the *Bilingual Kids: English-French, vol.3* Resource Book.

There Is, There Are
Il y a

chorus/*refrain :*

'*Il y a*', '*il y a*', '*il y a*'
In French we use '*il y a*'.
In English use 'there is', 'there are';
in French only '*il y a*'.

> *«Il y a», «il y a», «il y a»*
> *En français on dit «il y a».*
> *En anglais on dit «there is», «there are» ;*
> *en français seulement «il y a».*

In English if there's only one
'there is' is what we choose
but if we have two or more
'there are' is what we use.

> *Pour une seule chose en anglais*
> *«there is» nous choisissons*
> *mais pour deux choses ou plus*
> *«there are» nous utilisons.*

chorus/*refrain* :

'*Il y a*', '*il y a*', '*il y a*'
In French we use '*il y a*'.
In English use 'there is', 'there are';
in French only '*il y a*'.

>> *«Il y a», «il y a», «il y a»*
>> *En français on dit «il y a».*
>> *En anglais on dit «there is»,«there are» ;*
>> *en français seulement «il y a».*

Let's take time to build a fort.
We'll have lots of fun.
We'll use our tools carefully
and soon we will be done.

>> *Comme nous allons nous amuser*
>> *à construire un fort!*
>> *Utilisons bien nos outils*
>> *et vite nous aurons fini.*

Let's explore the tool box!
Explorons la boîte à outils!

There is a hammer in the box.
Il y a un marteau dans la boîte.

There is a saw in the box.
Il y a une scie dans la boîte.

There is a screwdriver in the box.
Il y a un tournevis dans la boîte.

There is a drill in the box.
Il y a une perceuse dans la boîte.

chorus/*refrain* :

'Il y a', 'il y a', 'il y a'
In French we use 'il y a'.
In English use 'there is', 'there are';
in French only 'il y a'.

«Il y a», «il y a», «il y a»
En français on dit «il y a».
En anglais on dit «there is», «there are» ;
en français seulement «il y a».

There are screws in the box.
Il y a des vis dans la boîte.

There are pliers in the box.
Il y a des pinces dans la boîte.

There are nuts in the box.
Il y a des écrous dans la boîte.

There are nails in the box.
Il y a des clous dans la boîte.

chorus/*refrain* :

'*Il y a*', '*il y a*', '*il y a*'
In French we use '*il y a*'.
In English use 'there is', 'there are';
in French only '*il y a*'.

> «*Il y a*», «*il y a*», «*il y a*»
> *En français on dit* «*il y a*».
> *En anglais on dit* «there is», «there are» ;
> *en français seulement* «*il y a*».

A Francophone Party
Une fête francophone

Let's have a party;
an awesome adjective party.
Let's have a party;
a splendid francophone party.

> *Célébrons une fête ;*
> *une fête avec des adjectifs.*
> *Célébrons une fête ;*
> *une fête francophone.*

chorus/*refrain* :

Adjectives describe the food we eat.
Adjectives describe the music's beat.
Adjectives describe the clothes we wear.
Adjectives describe nouns everywhere.

> *Les adjectifs pour ce que nous mangeons!*
> *Les adjectifs pour ce que nous dansons!*
> *Les adjectifs pour ce que nous portons!*
> *Les adjectifs pour décrire tous les noms!*

One, two, three...We'll eat:

French fries, roast chicken,
stuffed turkey, green peas;
and for dessert some sherbet
with a glass of iced tea.

Des pommes frites, du poulet rôti,
des petits pois, de la dinde farcie.
Pour dessert, du sorbet
avec un verre de thé glacé.

chorus/*refrain* :

Adjectives describe the food we eat.
Adjectives describe the music's beat.
Adjectives describe the clothes we wear.
Adjectives describe nouns everywhere.

Les adjectifs pour ce que nous mangeons!
Les adjectifs pour ce que nous dansons!
Les adjectifs pour ce que nous portons!
Les adjectifs pour décrire tous les noms!

One, two, three...We'll dance:

a romantic waltz,
a rhythmic cha-cha beat.
Around the world
francophones move their feet.

Une valse romantique,
un cha-cha bien rhythmé.
Autour du monde les francophones
aiment danser.

chorus/*refrain* :

Adjectives describe the food we eat.
Adjectives describe the music's beat.
Adjectives describe the clothes we wear.
Adjectives describe nouns everywhere.

Les adjectifs pour ce que nous mangeons!
Les adjectifs pour ce que nous dansons!
Les adjectifs pour ce que nous portons!
Les adjectifs pour décrire tous les noms!

One, two, three...We'll wear:

Elegant blouses
and orange skirts,
and wide shiny pants
with white shirts.

> *Des blouses élégantes*
> *et des jupes oranges,*
> *des pantalons flottants*
> *et des chemises blanches!*

chorus/*refrain* :

Adjectives describe the food we eat.
Adjectives describe the music's beat.
Adjectives describe the clothes we wear
Adjectives describe nouns everywhere!

> *Les adjectifs pour ce que nous mangeons!*
> *Les adjectifs pour ce que nous dansons!*
> *Les adjectifs pour ce que nous portons!*
> *Les adjectifs pour décrire tous les noms!*

My House is Your House
Faites comme chez vous!

chorus/*refrain* :

My house is your house.
You are all invited.
Come with your family.
Join in the fun.

We'll use possessive adjectives.
In French they'll agree
with the nouns they modify
and that they precede.

Faites comme chez vous.
Vous êtes les invités.
Venez avec votre famille.
Venez vous amuser!

Les adjectifs possessifs
en français s'accordent
avec les noms qu'ils modifient
et qu'ils précèdent.

I'll bring my mother.
You can bring your uncle.
He'll bring his cousin.
She'll bring her son.

Je viens avec ma mère.
Tu viens avec ton oncle.
Il vient avec sa cousine.
Elle vient avec son fils.

chorus/*refrain* :

We can bring our daughters.
You can bring your sisters
and finally they
can bring their dog.

Nous venons avec nos filles.
Vous venez avec vos sœurs
et enfin ils viennent
avec leur chien.

chorus/*refrain* :

Which One?
Lequel?

chorus/*refrain* :

They say that making choices isn't fun;
choosing between 'this one' or 'that one'.
In French there are even more
demonstrative adjectives:
> *ce, cet, cette,*
> *ce...ci* and *ce... là.*

> *On dit que choisir ce n'est pas facile,*
> *comme choisir entre «this one» ou «that one».*
> *En français il y a beaucoup plus*
> *d'adjectifs démonstratifs :*
> > *ce, cet, cette,*
> > *ce...ci et ce...là.*

When I go shopping
it really isn't fair.

This juice here, that juice there
or that juice way over there.
This ice-cream, that ice-cream
or that ice-cream over there.

It makes me feel frazzled
and like pulling out my hair!

Quand je fais les courses
ce n'est vraiment pas juste.

Ce jus-ci, ce jus-là
ou ce jus-là, là-bas.
Cette glace-ci, cette glace-là
ou cette glace-là, là-bas.

Cela me rend nerveuse
à m'en arracher les cheveux!

chorus/*refrain* :

They say that making choices isn't fun;
choosing between 'this one' or 'that one'.
In French there are even more
demonstrative adjectives:
    ce, cet, cette,
    ce...ci and *ce... là.*

On dit que choisir ce n'est pas facile,
comme choisir entre «this one» *ou* «that one».
En français il y a beaucoup plus
d'adjectifs démonstratifs :
    ce, cet, cette,
    ce...ci et ce...là.

When I go shopping
it really isn't fair.

This pizza here, that pizza there
or that pizza way over there!
This fruit here, that fruit there
or that fruit way over there!

It makes me feel frazzled
and like pulling out my hair!

Quand je fais les courses
ce n'est vraiment pas juste!

    Cette pizza-ci, cette pizza-là
    ou cette pizza-là là-bas.
    Ce fruit-ci, ce fruit-là
    ou ce fruit-là, là-bas.

Cela me rend nerveuse
à m'en arracher les cheveux!

chorus / *refrain* :

They say that making choices isn't fun;
choosing between 'this one' or 'that one'.
In French there are even more
demonstrative adjectives:
    ce, cet, cette,
    ce...ci and *ce... là.*

    On dit que choisir ce n'est pas facile,
    comme choisir entre «this one» *ou* «that one».
    En français il y a beaucoup plus
    d'adjectifs démonstratifs :
        ce, cet, cette,
        ce...ci et ce...là.

I'm Shopping
Je magasine

chorus:

I'm shopping. I'm shopping.
There's nothing going to stop me.
I'm shopping. I'm shopping
'til I drop.

I buy my clothes everywhere;
a little here, a little there.
Some of these, some of those;
I shop 'cause I like clothes.

I'm shopping. I'm shopping.
There's nothing going to stop me.
I'm shopping. I'm shopping
'til I drop.

refrain :

Je magasine. Je magasine.
Rien ne peut m'arrêter.
Je magasine. Je magasine
à Québec.

Partout, j'achète mes vêtements;
un peu ici, un peu là.
Ces vêtements-ci, ces vêtements-là ;
j'aime vraiment les vêtements.

Je magasine. Je magasine.
Rien ne peut m'arrêter.
Je magasine. Je magasine
à Québec.

Did you know?

In Quebec one says "je magasine" and in France one says "je fais les courses" or "je fais les magasins."

I want these shoes,
or those shoes,
or maybe those shoes
over there.
Make up your mind!

Je veux ces souliers-ci,
ou ces souliers-là,
ou peut-être ces souliers-là,
là-bas.
Décide-toi!

I want these boots,
or those boots,
or maybe those boots
over there.
Make up your mind!

Je veux ces bottes-ci,
ou ces bottes-là,
ou peut-être ces bottes-là,
là-bas.
Décide-toi!

I want these gloves,
or those gloves,
or maybe those gloves
over there.
    Make up your mind!

Je veux ces gants-ci,
ou ces gants-là,
ou peut-être ces gants-là,
là-bas.
    Décide-toi!

I want these sandals,
or those sandals,
or maybe those sandals
over there.
    Make up your mind

Je veux ces sandales-ci,
ou ces sandales-là,
ou peut-être ces sandales-là,
là-bas.
    Décide-toi!

chorus/*refrain*...

A Capital Idea!
Une idée majeure!

chorus/*refrain* :

Upper case, lower case.
Which letter do you choose?
Capitals in French follow
different rules.

> *Majuscules, minuscules.*
> *Quelle lettre est la bonne?*
> *Les majuscules en français*
> *sont différentes.*

Learn capitalization.
Come to the realization.
Rules are different.
It's best to discern.
Sit right down and
try to learn.

> *Pour devenir expert*
> *avec les majuscules*
> *il vaut mieux*
> *réaliser*
> *les différences.*
> *Apprenez!*

Upper case, lower case;
Which letter do you use?
Capitals in French follow
different rules.

Majuscules, minuscules
quelle lettre est la bonne?
Les majuscules en français,
sont différentes.

When writing in French
don't be surprised.
Days and months are
not capitalized.

And geographical names
are very different too:
'*l'océan Atlantique*'
and '*l'île Martinique*'.

Quand on écrit en français
ne soyez pas étonnés :
pas de majuscules
aux jours ni aux mois.

Les noms géographiques
sont très différents aussi :
«l'océan Atlantique»,
«l'île Martinique».

chorus/*refrain* :

Adjectives of nationality
and languages as well
are not capitalized:
'*français*' and '*japonais*'.

The trickiest rule of all
to remember
is for titles of books:
capitalize the first letter.

On ne met pas de majuscules
aux adjectifs de langue
et de nationnalité :
«français» et «japonais».

La règle la plus difficile
à ne pas oublier
dans le titre des livres :
mets une majuscule en premier.

chorus/*refrain* :

Ask your retailer about other excellent audio programs by teacher, Sara Jordan

Bilingual Songs™ Volumes 1-4

*** Parents' Choice Award Winner! ***

The perfect way to have fun while acquiring a second language. This series teaches the basic alphabet, counting to 100, days of the week, months of the year, colors, food, animals, parts of the body, clothing, family members, emotions, places in the community and the countryside, measurement, opposites, greetings, gender, articles, plural forms of nouns, adjectives, pronouns, adverbs of frequency, question words and much more! ENGLISH-FRENCH and ENGLISH-SPANISH

Songs and Activities for Early Learners™

Dynamic songs teach the alphabet, counting, parts of the body, members of the family, colors, shapes, fruit and more. Helps students of all ages to learn basic vocabulary easily. The kit includes a lyrics book with activities which teachers may reproduce for their classes. IN ENGLISH, FRENCH OR SPANISH

Thematic Songs for Learning Language™

Delightful collection of songs and activities teaching salutations, rooms of the house, pets, meals, food and silverware, transportation, communication, parts of the body, clothing, weather and prepositions. Great for ESL classes. The kit includes a lyrics book with activities teachers may reproduce for their classes. IN ENGLISH, FRENCH OR SPANISH

Reading Readiness Songs™

Comes with a lyrics book which includes helpful hints for parents and teachers. This great introduction to reading uses both phonics and whole language approaches. Topics covered include the alphabet, vowels, consonants, telling time, days of the week, seasons, the environment and more! VERSIONS IN ENGLISH, FRENCH OR SPANISH

Grammar Grooves vol. 1™

Ten songs that teach about nouns, pronouns, adjectives, verbs, tenses, adverbs and punctuation. Activities and puzzles, which may be reproduced, are included in the lyrics book to help reinforce learning even further. A complement of music tracks to the 10 songs is included for karaoke performances. Also great for music night productions. IN ENGLISH, FRENCH OR SPANISH

Funky Phonics®: Learn to Read Volumes 1-4

Blending the best in educational research and practice, Sara Jordan's four part series provides students with the strategies needed to decode words through rhyming, blending and segmenting. Teachers and parents love the lessons and activities while children will find the catchy, toe-tapping tunes fun. IN ENGLISH

Lullabies Around the World

*** Parents' Choice Award Winner! ***

Traditional lullabies sung by native singers with translated verses in English. Multicultural activities are included in the lyrics book. Includes a complement of music tracks for class performances. Pre-K - Grade 3   11 DIFFERENT LANGUAGES

Healthy Habits™

*** Directors' Choice Award Winner! ***

Songs and activities for Pre-K to Grade 3 covering nutrition, the food pyramid, anatomy, dental hygiene, personal and fire safety. The lyrics book which accompanies the recording has activities which can be reproduced for a class. A complement of music-only tracks works well for performances. IN ENGLISH

The Presidents' Rap®

from Washington to George W. Bush. The legends of the American Presidents live on in classical, swing, dixie, pop and rap music. A musical treasure trove of tid-bits of information on each President. Very popular among teachers wanting to put on musical shows in their school. IN ENGLISH

The Math Unplugged™ Series

Available for Addition, Subtraction, Division and Multiplication. Tuneful songs teach kids the basic math facts. Repetitive, musical and fun. A great resource. Each audio kit includes a lyrics book with worksheet pages which may be reproduced. IN ENGLISH

Check out these great Resource Books full of reproducible activities and exercises for the classroom.

Bilingual Kids™ Volumes 1-4

Reproducible black-line thematic lessons and exercises, based on Bilingual Songs, teach the basic alphabet, counting to 100, days of the week, months of the year, colors, food, animals, parts of the body, clothing, family members, emotions, places in the community and the countryside, measurement, opposites, greetings, gender, articles, plural forms of nouns, adjectives, pronouns, adverbs of frequency, question words and much more! ENGLISH-FRENCH and ENGLISH-SPANISH

French for Kids: Beginning Lessons

Reproducible, black-line thematic lessons and exercises in Spanish, based on *Español para principiantes*, teach the alphabet, numbers, days of the week, opposites, colors, family members, body parts and much more! Lessons are enhanced with information about Hispanic culture. 64 pages. Beginner level. IN FRENCH

French for Kids: Thematic Lessons

Reproducible, black-line thematic lessons and exercises in Spanish, based on *Canciones temáticas*, teach common expressions, salutations, time, modes of transportation, pets, prepositions and much more! Lessons are enhanced with information on Hispanic culture. 64 pages. Beginner level. IN FRENCH

Thematic French Lessons & Activities

French across the curriculum! Liven up your classes all year long with these reproducible French lessons and activities based on holidays and seasons. Includes: dictations, conjugation exercises practicing –er, –ir, –re verbs, avoir and être in the present tense, word searches, crossword puzzles, art projects and brainteasers. 64 pages. IN FRENCH

Please visit our web site, a great meeting place for kids, teachers and parents on the Internet.

www.SongsThatTeach.com

www.Aprendecantando.com

For help finding a retailer near you contact
Sara Jordan Publishing 1-800-567-7733